The Split History of the
ATTACK ON PEARL HARBOR:

JAPANESE PERSPECTIVE

BY STEVEN OTFINOSKI

CONTENT CONSULTANT:
Tim Solie
Adjunct Professor of History
Minnesota State University, Mankato

COMPASS POINT BOOKS
a capstone imprint

ABOUT THE AUTHOR

Steven Otfinoski has written more than 180 books for young readers. Three of his nonfiction books have been named Books for the Teen Age by the New York Public Library. Steve also enjoys teaching college English and creative writing. He lives in Connecticut with his wife.

SOURCE NOTES

American Perspective:

Page 5, line 12: Richard Goldstein. "Kermit Tyler, Player of a Fateful, if Minor, Role in Pearl Harbor Attack, Dies at 96." *The New York Times*. 25 Feb. 2010. 13 Oct. 2017. http://www.nytimes.com/2010/02/26/us/26tyler.html?mcubz=0

Page 6, line 11: "A People at War." National Archives. 13 Oct. 2017. https://www.archives.gov/exhibits/a_people_at_war/prelude_to_war/prelude_to_war.html

Page 10, line 4: D.C. Godwin. "Meritorious Conduct of a Seaman." USS *Maryland* (BB-46). Paducah, Ky.: Turner Publishing Company, 1997, p. 65.

Page 11, line 10: Joy Waldron Jasper, James P. Delgado, and Jim Adams. *The USS Arizona: The Ship, the Men, the Pearl Harbor Attack, and the Symbol that Aroused America*. New York: St. Martin's Press, 2001, p.129.

Page 12, line 10: "Carl Carson, Survivor, USS *Arizona*." Military.com. 13 Oct. 2017. http://www.military.com/Content/MoreContent?file=carson01

Page 14, line 20: Jasmine Willis. "Community Remembers Pearl Harbor." *Observer*. 8 Dec. 2013. 20 Oct., 2017. http://content.observertoday.com/news/page-one/2013/12/community-remembers-pearl-harbor/

Page 20, line 24: T. J. Keating, ed. *Joint and National Intelligence Support to Military Operations: Joint Publication 2-01, October 7, 2004*, p. V-12.

Page 23, line 19: Stephen Bower Young. *Trapped at Pearl Harbor: Escape from Battleship* Oklahoma. Annapolis, Md.: Naval Institute Press, 1991, Ch. 23, p. 2.

Page 25, line 22: Matthew C. Whitaker. *Peace Be Still: Modern Black America from World War II to Barack Obama*. Lincoln, Neb.: University of Nebraska Press, 2013, p.15.

Page 27, line 8: Katie Mettler. "75 Years Later, Remembering FDR's Day of 'Infamy,' a Phrase that Almost Wasn't." *The Washington Post*. 7 Dec. 2016. 13 Oct. 2017. https://www.washingtonpost.com/news/morning-mix/wp/2016/12/07/75-years-later-remembering-fdrs-day-of-infamy-a-phrase-that-almost-wasnt/?utm_term=.038c437cc325

Page 27, line 16: Lily Rothman. "This Is What Eleanor Roosevelt Said to America's Women on the Day of Pearl Harbor." *Time*. 7 Dec. 2016. 13 Oct. 2017. http://time.com/4584910/eleanor-roosevelt-pearl-harbor/

Page 27, line 23: Franklin D. Roosevelt. "Speech by Franklin D. Roosevelt, New York (Transcript)." December 8, 1941. Library of Congress. 13 Oct. 2017. https://www.loc.gov/resource/afc1986022.afc1986022_ms2201/?st=text

Japanese Perspective:

Page 13, sidebar, line 20: Laurie Collier Hilstrom. *Defining Moments: The Attack on Pearl Harbor*. Detroit, Mich.: Omnigraphics, 2009, p. 126.

Page 15, line 19: Priscilla Roberts, ed. *Voices of World War II: Contemporary Accounts of Daily Life*. Santa Barbara, Calif.: Greenwood, 2012, p. 37.

Page 16, line 6: Henry Scott Stokes. "40 Years Later, Japanese Pilot Recalls Pearl Harbor." *The New York Times*. 7 Dec. 1981. 13 Oct. 2017. http://www.nytimes.com/1981/12/07/world/40-years-later-japanese-pilot-recalls-pearl-harbora.html

Page 18, line 8: *Voices of World War II: Contemporary Accounts of Daily Life*, p. 37.

Page 18, line 16: Warren R. Schmidt. "Lieutenant Zenji Abe: A Japanese Pilot Remembers." *World War II Magazine*. May 2001. 13 Oct. 2017. http://www.historynet.com/lieutenant-zenji-abe-a-japanese-pilot-remembers.htm

Page 18, line 21: Ibid.

Page 21, line 2: Ibid.

Page 22, line 7: Walter Lord. *Day of Infamy*. New York: Henry Holt and Company, 1957, p. 181.

Page 23, line 7: Don Nardo, ed. *Pearl Harbor*. San Diego: Greenhaven Press, 2003, p. 28.

Page 23, line 10: Craig Shirley. *December 1941: 31 Days that Changed America and Saved the World*. Nashville, Tenn.: Thomas Nelson, 2011, p. 159.

Page 29, line 19: Chris Huberthal. "U.S., Japanese WWII Vets Honor Fallen with Blackened Canteen Spirits." *America's Navy*. 6 Dec. 2015. 13 Oct. 2017. http://www.navy.mil/submit/display.asp?story_id=92295

Table of Contents

SHARED RESOURCES

CHAPTER 1: A RISKY PLAN

Flight Commander Mitsuo Fuchida checked his watch as he led the formation of 183 planes toward the northern shore of Oahu. It was 7:40 a.m. Hawaiian time. They had been flying an hour and a half since leaving the aircraft carriers that had transported them from Japan. Fuchida scanned the break in the clouds below for a sign of land. The long, white curl of breaking surf came into view. They had reached their goal. Fuchida steered his plane to the west coast of Oahu and looked down at the crystal blue waters of Pearl Harbor, home of the U.S. Pacific Fleet. Seven of the eight battleships stationed at Pearl Harbor were lined up neatly below, gleaming in the bright morning sun.

Shortly after this photo was taken on December 7, 1941, the Japanese planes left the aircraft carrier and headed for Pearl Harbor.

The time had finally arrived for the attack they had been planning for many months. Now Fuchida had one last decision to make. If the Americans were taken by surprise, he was to fire his signal gun once for the pilots behind him to see. Then the torpedo planes would attack first, going for the battleships. They would be followed by the level bombers and finally the dive-bombers. However, if the Americans were prepared for the attack, Fuchida would fire twice, meaning "surprise lost." Then the dive-bombers and fighter planes would attack the airfields first to prevent the American pilots from taking to the skies for a counterattack.

The problem was that Fuchida had no information as to whether the Americans were aware of the strike. Reconnaissance planes had been sent on ahead to report on the ground conditions, but he had received no word from them. From what he could see from the air, the Americans were completely unaware of their arrival, so he fired the signal gun once through his open window. A black plume of smoke drifted across the blue sky. The dive-bombers saw the signal and got into formation for their attack. But there was no response from the fighter planes. Had they not seen the signal? Fuchida decided to fire again. This time the fighter planes saw the smoke, but so did the planes that had seen the first signal. They mistook it to mean "surprise lost"—that the Americans were ready for them. All the planes prepared to attack at once. Fuchida decided that it hardly mattered. The attack had begun; that was all that mattered.

The attack, which began at 7:55 a.m. on December 7, 1941, had been in the planning stages for nearly two years. It was the brainchild of Naval Commander Admiral Isoroku Yamamoto. He was part of a military that wanted to show the United States and the world that Japan could conquer its neighbors in Asia and build an empire as mighty as any in the West.

Yamamoto felt that the only way Japan could achieve this goal was to eliminate the most powerful obstacle in its path—the United States. By destroying the U.S. Pacific Fleet stationed at Pearl Harbor, the Japanese would have at least six months before the United States could rebuild its naval power and counterattack.

Yamamoto first presented his daring plan to other military leaders in early 1940, but they thought the plan was too risky and dangerous. Yamamoto agreed that there was risk involved, but he remained confident that it could work. He had spent several years in the United States as a young man and felt the Americans would be completely crushed by the loss of their fleet.

In October Yamamoto presented his plan again at a naval conference. All but one of the navy's admirals still opposed it. On October 17 Yamamoto and his entire staff threatened to resign if the plan was not accepted. The government leaders finally gave in. They could not afford to lose one of their greatest military leaders. Also, Yamamoto had a strong ally in Commander Genda Minoru, whom he put in charge of air power for the attack. The military leaders were at first skeptical about primarily using airplanes to attack Pearl Harbor. But they were gradually convinced that an attack from the air would be more effective and lethal than an attack on the water with warships.

For months, Minoru refined the attack plan with Yamamoto and trained the pilots who would participate. Meanwhile, Japanese representatives in America were told to continue negotiations with the United States to ease growing tensions over Japanese aggression in China and elsewhere. Japan's leaders wanted to make the Americans think they were seeking peace when they were secretly preparing for war. By mid-November 1941 the time had come to put Yamamoto's daring plan into action.

ADMIRAL ISOROKU YAMAMOTO

Admiral Isoroku Yamamoto was the architect of
Japan's attack on Pearl Harbor. A year after
graduating from the Japanese Naval Academy in
1904, Yamamoto saw action and was wounded in the
Russo-Japanese War (1904-1905).

Yamamoto spent nearly
a decade in the United
States between 1919 and
1928. He learned English
at Harvard University
and later served as
an admiral's aide in
the United States.
His low opinion of the
abilities of U.S. naval
officers convinced him
that a sneak attack
on Pearl Harbor
would be successful.

Isoroku Yamamoto

On his return to
Japan, Yamamoto worked
his way up to becoming
one of the most important aviation officers in
the Naval Air Corps. As commander in chief of the
Combined Japanese Fleet, Yamamoto believed
aircraft carriers were more effective weapons
in war than battleships. Although his attack
on Pearl Harbor was seen as a great victory,
he later lost important battles against the
Americans at Midway Island and the Solomon
Islands, due in part to battle plans that were
too complicated to carry out successfully. During
a tour of Japanese bases in the South Pacific in
April 1943, American forces shot down Yamamoto's
plane, and he was killed. He did not live to see
Japan's total defeat more than two years later.

CHAPTER 2

BY AIR AND BY SEA

At 6 a.m. on November 26, 1941, an enormous naval force left Hitokappu Bay in the Kuril Islands of Japan for a 3,500-mile (5,633-kilometer) journey across the Pacific to the island of Oahu in Hawaii. The impressive fleet, which included six aircraft carriers, nine destroyers, two battleships, two heavy cruisers, and one light cruiser, carried 353 planes. The ships would not arrive at the takeoff point until December 7, the designated date of the attack. This date was chosen because the days before it coincided with the full moon, which would make night navigation easier. December 7 was also a Sunday, a day when most personnel on the American base would be off duty and resting, totally unprepared for a surprise attack.

Aircraft carriers

WARSHIPS WITH A FLIGHT DECK WHERE
AIRPLANES CAN LAND AND LAUNCH

Battleships

HEAVILY ARMED WARSHIPS EQUIPPED
WITH POWERFUL WEAPONS

Cruisers

LARGE, FAST, ARMED WARSHIPS,
SMALLER THAN BATTLESHIPS

Destroyers

SMALL, FAST, WELL-ARMED WARSHIPS
THAT OFTEN SUPPORT LARGER SHIPS

*Five two-man minisubs were involved in the attack on Pearl Harbor.
This one washed up on shore in Hawaii on December 7.*

But there was another component to the attack besides the
planes. Full-sized submarines carrying five minisubs, each with
two men and two torpedoes aboard, had left their naval bases
days before the fleet. The minisubs were left just 7 miles (11 km)
from the entrance of Pearl Harbor in the early morning hours of
December 7. Unlike full-sized subs, the minisubs could navigate the
shallow waters of the harbor to sneak up on American warships.
They would fire their torpedoes once the air attack began.

The fleet did not receive its final orders to attack until
December 2. By then the ships had experienced just about every
kind of weather imaginable. The strongest winds and most

destructive weather occurred on the morning of December 7.
As the fleet reached its destination—a point 200 miles (322 km)
north of Oahu—the seas were so rough that the pilots had to
cling to their aircraft to avoid being tossed into the ocean. Then
at 5 a.m. Vice Admiral Chuichi Nagumo, commander of the fleet,
received distressing news: Reconnaissance planes were unable
to locate the American aircraft carriers, the main targets of the
attack. Apparently, they had all been sent out to sea. Nagumo was
disappointed but decided it was too late to stop the attack. They
would have to be satisfied with their secondary target—the eight
U.S. battleships docked in the harbor. Nagumo could only hope that
the aircraft carriers would return to base before the attack ended.

Shortly after 6 a.m. the first planes took off for Pearl Harbor
from the carrier *Akagi*. An hour before the planes reached their

destination, the first
encounter had already
taken place at Pearl
Harbor. The U.S.
destroyer *Ward* had
spotted the short
observation tower of one
of Japan's minisubs that
rose above the surface
of the water. The USS
Ward fired a torpedo at
the unidentified sub in its

The carrier Akagi *brought Japanese planes
across the Pacific to attack Pearl Harbor.*

waters, blowing it to pieces. A report on this incident was sent to U.S. Fleet Commander Husband Kimmel, but he waited to take further action until he could verify the accuracy of the report. His reason was that there had recently been many false sightings of submarines off Pearl Harbor.

AIR COMMANDER MITSUO FUCHIDA

Mitsuo Fuchida served his country valiantly throughout the war and was wounded at the Battle of Midway Island in June 1942. On that day Fuchida was aboard the *Akagi*, which had served as an aircraft carrier in the Pearl Harbor attack. At Midway, American forces sank the *Akagi*, but Fuchida was rescued before the ship went down.

Mitsuo Fuchida

After the war Fuchida converted to Christianity and spread a message of love and peace throughout the United States and Europe. He also wrote several books about his experiences, including *From Pearl Harbor to Calvary*. "I would give anything to [undo] my actions at Pearl Harbor, but it is impossible," he wrote. "Instead, I now work at striking the death-blow to the basic hatred which infests the human heart and causes such tragedies."

CHAPTER 3

TORA! TORA! TORA!

As Commander Fuchida prepared to launch the attack on Pearl Harbor, he had his radioman send out a message to his superiors back on the *Akagi*. "Tora! Tora! Tora!" it read.

Tora means "tiger" in Japanese, but the word was actually an acronym for *totsugeki raigeki*, meaning "lightning attack." He was telling the military leaders that they had achieved complete surprise over the Americans and were about to attack. The *Akagi* conveyed this news back to the war council in Tokyo.

From there the message was relayed to Japanese units waiting near other targets—British colonies Hong Kong and Malaya, the Philippines, and America's Pacific island territories Guam and Wake Island. This was their signal to attack those locations as well. It was all part of a widespread campaign of which Pearl Harbor was the centerpiece.

Back at Battleship Row, the attack went forward with frightening precision. The torpedo bombers flew low over the battleships, launching their missiles just 50 feet (15 m) above the harbor. Once the torpedoes hit the water, they took off on their own power and struck the ships where they were most vulnerable, below the waterline. Then the dive-bombers moved in and fired on the ships' topsides. They completely blanketed the decks with machine-gun fire, killing crew members racing for cover.

The fighter planes focused on the airfields. They fired at the neat rows of planes lined up on the ground, destroying as many as possible so that American pilots couldn't launch a counterattack. As crewmen and pilots emerged from hangars and other buildings, the Japanese pilots shot them down where they stood.

Fuchida and his bombers had finished their first assault and were preparing to fly over again when the unexpected happened. "[T]here was a colossal explosion in Battleship Row," Fuchida later recalled. "A huge column of dark red smoke rose to 1,000 meters [3,280 feet]. . . . The shock wave was felt even in my plane, several miles away from the harbor."

What Fuchida experienced was the death blow to the USS *Arizona*. A direct hit from a bomb ignited the ammunition magazine below deck, creating a monstrous explosion. The fiery wreck of the *Arizona* sank within minutes, taking many of the 1,500 crew members to a watery grave.

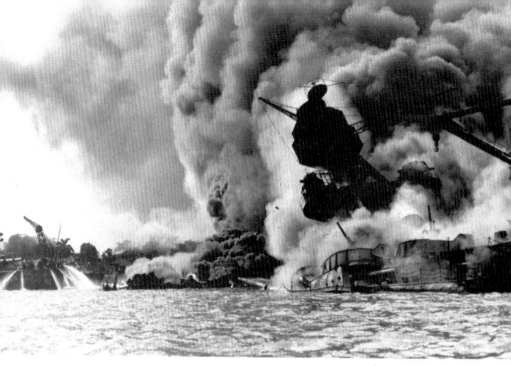

The USS Arizona *sank in less than 10 minutes when its forward magazine exploded after it was struck by a bomb.*

Another Japanese pilot, Yoshio Shiga, was leading a formation of fighter planes called Japanese Zeroes when he suddenly found himself the target of antiaircraft fire. A few bold Americans on the ground had begun firing with whatever weapons they could find. Shiga had experienced enemy fire before when fighting the Chinese a year earlier. "Compared with the Chinese fire, the American firepower was enormous," he later wrote, "The clouds and fire-puffs in the sky looked like a basket of flowers. It was really frightening."

JAPANESE ZEROES

Fighter planes known as Japanese Zeroes were
the pride of Japan's air force. In the beginning
of the war, they were unmatched in power and
speed by any other planes. The single seat,
low-wing planes were first developed and tested
in 1939 and went into combat in China the
following year. They could reach top speeds of
350 miles (563 km) per hour at nearly 20,000 feet
(6,100 m). They carried two machine guns and
two 20-millimeter cannons in their wings. They
could also carry two 132-pound (60 kg) bombs
under their wings. Besides this, the Zeroes could
fly longer than many other planes because of a
second 94-gallon (356-liter) extension tank that,
when empty, could be dropped from the plane.

The Zeroes' supremacy in the skies ended
later in the war when the United States began
producing better small fighter planes that could
match the Zeroes in combat.

The Americans were unable to stand up to the continuous attack of the Japanese, so resistance from them was scattered and infrequent. In less than 40 minutes, the Japanese had done massive damage. They hit all seven battleships docked in Battleship Row and destroyed or damaged more than 100 planes on the airfields. Then, as suddenly as they had struck, the Japanese planes departed. Fuchida stayed behind to survey the destruction with great satisfaction. "Pearl Harbor and the air bases had been pretty well wrecked. . . . The imposing naval array of an hour before was gone," he said. "Antiaircraft fire had become greatly intensified, but . . . I saw no enemy fighter planes. Our command of the air was unchallenged."

Before the first wave of planes had left Pearl Harbor, a second wave of 167 more planes was departing from the aircraft carriers. Squadron leader Lieutenant Zenji Abe was piloting one of these planes. "All the carriers were anthills of activity," Abe recalled. "Planes were lifted from the hangars and readied for the takeoff of the second wave, which was to follow the first by one hour."

Like many of the Japanese pilots, Abe did not know what to expect. He wondered if perhaps the Americans had had enough time in between attacks to mount a strong defense. "Their decks . . . danced with the flashes of antiaircraft guns that all seemed to be pointed at me," Abe later recalled. "I caught sight of another formation of bombers diving below on our right, and I no longer felt alone. One by one they [dove] until the last had gone into his dive, and then it was our turn."

Lieutenant Zenji Abe moments before taking off for
Pearl Harbor in his fighter plane

By 10 a.m. it was over. The planes of the second wave circled in the sky and began the flight back to the waiting aircraft carriers. Only one plane remained behind. It was piloted by Commander Fuchida who took photograph after photograph of the devastation below. It was a record of achievement to share with his superiors aboard the *Akagi.*

CHAPTER 4

A FATEFUL DECISION

By 11:15 a.m. planes from the second wave were starting to return to the aircraft carriers. To shorten the flight for the returning pilots, the carriers had moved steadily in the direction of Oahu. Within an hour, nearly all the planes were back, although some were missing. The high command examined the losses: 29 planes, all 5 minisubs, and 55 men. All the men on the minisubs were assumed dead, although they didn't know yet that one sub crew member, Kazuo Sakamaki, had been captured. In comparison, 2,335 American servicemen and civilians had been killed and 1,143 were wounded.

Even though their losses were minimal, the surviving pilots and airmen were grateful to be alive. "I entered the tiny room and began to remove my flight clothes," Lieutenant Abe remembered. "In the center of my otherwise clean desk lay the envelope containing my will, addressed to my father. Suddenly, my spirits lifted. It was good to be alive."

But while the airmen were settling in for the long voyage back to Japan, a new drama was unfolding on the bridge of the *Akagi*. Some leading officers, Fuchida among them, were arguing to return to Pearl Harbor for a third time to inflict further destruction. They pointed out to Fleet Commander Nagumo that there were vital facilities they had missed on the first two attacks. These included the fuel tanks containing millions of gallons of oil to run the ships and planes, as well as the repair facilities where the damaged ships

Had the Japanese succeeded in bombing the circular white fuel tanks during the Pearl Harbor attack, the devastation would have been much worse.

could be repaired and put back into action. And then there were the three missing aircraft carriers that were out to sea. They may well have returned by the time the Japanese struck again.

Nagumo listened respectfully to these arguments. Then he turned to his chief of staff, Rear Admiral Rynasuke Kusaka, who shook his head. He was not convinced that it was worth going back again. "The attack is terminated," he said flatly. "We are withdrawing." Nagumo agreed. The other officers accepted their superiors' decision and soon the fleet was heading back to Japan.

Some historians feel the decision not to go back for a third attack was a fatal one. They point out that if the Japanese had destroyed the Americans' fuel supply and repair facilities, it would have taken several more months for the U.S. Pacific Fleet to recover. This would have given the Japanese more time to invade Southeast Asia and other important islands in the Pacific. It might have given the Japanese a better chance of prolonging, and possibly winning, the war in Asia.

However, other historians and writers argue that the high command was wise not to go back for a final strike. They point out that it would have taken hours to organize a third wave of planes. Those planes would not have reached Oahu until after nightfall, and an attack in the darkness would have been much more dangerous. If, on the other hand, they waited until the next day, December 8, to launch another attack, they might have faced an American force prepared and ready for them. By then, a ground defense might have been organized and the undamaged planes would have been ready to launch a counterattack. And if, as the leaders hoped, the aircraft carriers had returned by then, they could have provided a launching pad for these American aircraft.

Incomplete as it was, Japan's victory was a cause for national celebration back home. The front page of the *Japan Times and Advertiser* boasted the banner headline "U.S. Pacific Fleet Is Wiped Out!" War Minister Hideki Tojo went on national radio to announce the victory and proclaim that Japan was at war with the United States. "I hereby promise you," he declared, "that Japan will win final victory."

Meanwhile, back in Washington, D.C., Japanese diplomats and officials at their embassy were frantically fueling a bonfire on the back lawn with thousands of documents and codebooks. A huge crowd of Americans stood on the sidewalk outside the embassy and booed and hissed as they watched the smoke from the bonfire rise into the chilly December sky.

JAPANESE AMBASSADOR KICHISABURO NOMURA

Admiral Kichisaburo Nomura retired from the
Japanese Navy in 1937. He became ambassador to the
United States in November 1940. Nomura was friendly
toward the Americans and tried to negotiate a
peaceful settlement with the United States in the
hopes of preventing the two countries from going to
war. But his superiors refused to support him, and
while they prepared for war, they kept him in the
dark about the Pearl Harbor attack.

Nomura and a colleague kept a scheduled meeting
with U.S. Secretary of State Cordell Hull after the
attack had begun. Hull, who had been told about
the attack before the meeting, dismissed them
coldly. During the meeting, Nomura was tasked with
delivering Japan's declaration of war.

Nomura was held in Virginia for the next six
months, and then he returned to Japan. He held
no formal position during the war but reentered
government in the 1950s. Nomura was a serious
candidate to head the Defense Agency in the late
1950s, but he refused to take the position. He felt
it should be filled by a civilian, not a former
military man. A man of peace in a time of war,
Nomura died in 1964.

Cordell Hull and Admiral Nomura before the war

CHAPTER 5

RISING SUN, SETTING SUN

The Japanese saw the attack on Pearl Harbor as the beginning of a glorious war against the Allies. But it turned out to be their biggest mistake. They had misjudged the Americans' ability to repair the damage to their ships and planes. In fact, the Americans came back stronger than ever. More importantly, the Japanese misjudged the strength and perseverance of the United States. Many Japanese leaders, like Yamamoto, thought the Americans would be so stunned by the attack that they would offer little resistance as Japan conquered much of Asia and the Pacific.

On the contrary, the attack united Americans, even those who had wanted to stay out of the war. They were more determined than ever to defeat Japan and its allies, Germany and Italy.

At first the Japanese held the upper hand. Fresh from their success on December 7, their forces rolled across the Pacific, scoring victory after victory on sea and land. But the American war machine was gearing up too.

On June 7, 1942, the Americans gained an important victory at Midway Island. The Battle of Midway was a turning point in the war in the Pacific. American dive-bombers sank four Japanese aircraft carriers, all of which had taken part in the attack on Pearl Harbor nearly seven months earlier. From that point on, the Japanese were on the defensive, trying to hold on to the territory they had conquered. But the Americans relentlessly

The Japanese heavy cruiser Mikuma *sank during the Battle of Midway.*

closed in, retaking those islands and moving closer and closer toward Japan and an ultimate victory.

The war in Europe ended with Germany's surrender in May 1945, but the war in the Pacific continued. President Harry Truman, who became the leader of the United States when Franklin Roosevelt died in April, considered launching a land invasion of Japan. But he felt a land invasion could cost hundreds of thousands of lives, both Japanese and American. Instead Truman made the decision to attack Japan with a devastating new weapon recently developed by the United States — the atomic bomb.

On August 6, 1945, a U.S. plane dropped an atomic bomb on the Japanese city of Hiroshima. The blast killed at least 78,000 people. For two days, no word of surrender came from Japanese leaders. Then on August 9, the United States dropped a second atomic bomb, this time on the city of Nagasaki, killing another 40,000 people. Japan surrendered within a week.

When the atomic bomb exploded, an enormous mushroom-shaped cloud formed over the city of Nagasaki.

The war that had started so well for Japan ended in its total ruin. After Japan's surrender the rays around the rising sun were removed from its national flag. Although symbolically the rising sun of Japan had set, the nation itself would soon rise again.

American troops occupied Japan until 1952. The United States demilitarized Japan and helped establish a new democratic government. It also offered financial and economic aid to bring Japan back into the brotherhood of modern, democratic nations. By the mid-1950s, Japan's economy had returned to its prewar level, a remarkable achievement. Today, Japan is a major industrial power, one dedicated to peace, not war.

Mamoru Shigemitsu, Japan's minister of foreign affairs, signed a surrender document on September 2, 1945.

THE BLACKENED CANTEEN

Each year American World War II veterans gather at Pearl Harbor for a ceremony that has brought them together with the Japanese veterans who were once their sworn enemies. It is called the Blackened Canteen ceremony.

A canteen filled with whiskey was discovered in the wreckage of two American B-29 bombers that had collided during a raid on Japan in 1945. The 23 Americans who died in the crash and the Japanese civilians who were killed in the bombing were buried together.

Each year near the anniversary of the Pearl Harbor attack, Dr. Hiroya Sugano, director of the Zero Fighter Admirers' Club, brings the canteen from Japan to the USS *Arizona* Memorial at Pearl Harbor. Then an American and a Japanese World War II vet together pour whiskey from the canteen into the waters above the sunken battleship. It is a sign of unity for the former enemies. "The whiskey is really the water of life . . . ," said *Arizona* Memorial historian Daniel Martinez. "[A]s it falls into the water, it's a way of extending the hand of friendship, forgiveness, and peace."

INDEX

SELECT BIBLIOGRAPHY

Arroyo, Ernest. *Pearl Harbor*. New York: MetroBooks, 2001.

Gillon, Steven M. *Pearl Harbor: FDR Leads the Nation into War*. New York: Basic Books, 2011.

Hillstrom, Laurie Collier. *Defining Moment: The Attack on Pearl Harbor*. Detroit, Mich.: Omnigraphics, 2009.

Nardo, Don, ed. *Pearl Harbor*. San Diego.: Greenhaven Press, 2003.

Shirley, Craig. *December 1941: 31 Days that Changed America and Saved the World*. Nashville, Tenn.: Thomas Nelson, 2011.

Stille, Mark. "Yamamoto and the Planning for Pearl Harbor." *The History Reader*. http://www.thehistoryreader.com/modern-history/yamamoto-planning-pearl-harbor/

Stokes, Henry Scott. "Forty Years Later, Japanese Pilot Recalls Pearl Harbor." *The New York Times*. http://www.nytimes.com/1981/12/07/world/d/40-years-later-japanese-pilot-recalls-pearl-harbora.html

Willmott, H.P. *Pearl Harbor*. London: Cassell Co., 2001.

FURTHER READING

Allen, Thomas B. *Remember Pearl Harbor: American and Japanese Survivors Tell Their Stories*. Washington, D.C.: National Geographic, 2015.

Edwards, Sue Bradford. *The Bombing of Pearl Harbor*. Minneapolis, Minn.: Abdo Publishing, 2016.

Fitzgerald, Stephanie. *Pearl Harbor*. North Mankato, Minn: Capstone Press, 2018.

Johnson, Robin. *Pearl Harbor*. New York: Crabtree Publishing Company, 2014.

CRITICAL THINKING QUESTIONS

1. There were warnings about the coming attack on Pearl Harbor. What were they, and why do you think that they were ignored by the United States? Use evidence from the text to support your answer.

2. What reasons did some Japanese officers have for wanting to attack Pearl Harbor a third time? Why did their superiors not agree? Based on the evidence and expert opinions, do you think the Japanese made a wise decision?

3. If the Japanese had not attacked Pearl Harbor and had avoided conflict with the United States, do you think the U.S. would have stayed out of World War II? Why or why not? Give reasons for your answer based on the text and your own thinking.

1937

The Second Sino-Japanese War begins

1937-1938

During December 1937 and January 1938 an estimated 300,000 Chinese soldiers and civilians are killed when the Japanese Imperial Army invades the city of Nanking, China; the event becomes known as the Nanking Massacre

1939

SEPTEMBER 1: Germany invades Poland

SEPTEMBER 3: World War II begins when Great Britain, France, Australia, and New Zealand declare war on Germany

1940

SEPTEMBER 27: Japan, Germany, and Italy sign an agreement forming the Axis Powers

8:10 A.M.: The USS Arizona is hit by a bomb and explodes in a fireball; the ship quickly sinks, taking 1,177 men to a watery grave

8:30 A.M.: The first wave of the attack ends

8:54 A.M.: Another wave of Japanese planes begins a second assault on Pearl Harbor

10:00 A.M.: Japanese planes head back to their aircraft carriers; the attack is over

DECEMBER 8: The United States and several other countries declare war on Japan

DECEMBER 11: Germany and Italy declare war on the United States

1945

AUGUST 6: A U.S. plane drops an atomic bomb on the Japanese city of Hiroshima, killing at least 78,000 people

AUGUST 9: The United States drops a second atomic bomb, this time on the city of Nagasaki, Japan, killing 40,000 people

SEPTEMBER 2: Japan surrenders and World War II is over

TIMELINE

1853

U.S. battleships commanded by Commodore Matthew Perry force Japan to sign a trade agreement with the United States

1894-1895

Japan defeats China in the First Sino-Japanese War; this victory demonstrates Japan's transformation militarily as a world power

1904-1905

Japan defeats Russia in the Russo-Japanese War; in doing so, Japan becomes the first Asian country to defeat a European power in modern times

1921-1922

Several countries meet at the Washington Naval Conference and sign multiple treaties; these treaties set limits on the manufacture of weapons and warships in Japan and other countries

1931

Japan invades the Chinese province of Manchuria

1941

JULY 24: Japan invades French Indochina (present-day Vietnam) with the goal of taking over all of Southeast Asia and the Phillipines

AUGUST 1: The United States issues an embargo on exports of oil and fuel to Japan

SEPTEMBER: The U.S. Navy intercepts a coded message from Tokyo asking the Japanese consulate in Hawaii to note the locations of U.S. warships at Pearl Harbor

DECEMBER 7:

6:10 A.M.: Japanese fighter planes take off from aircraft carriers and head toward Pearl Harbor

7:02 A.M.: Using radar, George Elliott and Joseph Lockard notice what appears to be a large group of aircraft headed toward Pearl Harbor; they call Fort Shafter and are told not to worry about it

7:33 A.M.: U.S. Army Chief of Staff George Marshall receives a message intended for the Japanese consulate telling him to break ties with the Americans and destroy his important documents; Marshall tries to warn authorities in Hawaii, but the message doesn't arrive in time

7:55 A.M.: The attack on Pearl Harbor begins

GLOSSARY

AMBASSADOR—a government official who represents his or her country in a foreign country

ANNEX—to incorporate into a country or state

BRIDGE—the control center high on the forward section of a ship

CASUALTIES—people killed, wounded, or missing in battle or war

COMMONWEALTH—a country that rules itself but maintains ties to a larger nation

DRY DOCK—a dock where the water can be drained to repair ships

EMBARGO—an act by a government stopping trade to or from another country

EMBASSY—place where the government representatives of another country work

INFAMY—a lasting, widespread, and deep-rooted evil reputation brought about by something criminal, shocking, or brutal

INTERCEPT—to stop the movement of an object

MAGAZINE—a room aboard a ship where ammunition and explosives are stored

NEGOTIATIONS—discussions in order to come to an agreement

RECONNAISSANCE—scouting an area

SUFFOCATE—to die from lack of air

INTERNET SITES

Use FactHound to find Internet sites related to this book.

Visit www.facthound.com

Just type in 9780756556914 and go.